Touring with Toby

• Respecting Your Country •

By T. M. Merk

The Child's World®
childsworld.com

Published by The Child's World®
1980 Lookout Drive • Mankato, MN 56003-1705
800-599-READ • www.childsworld.com

Photographs: wavebreakmedia/Shutterstock.com,
cover, 1, 11, 19; Orhan Cam/Shutterstock.com, 5;
Jon Bilous/Shutterstock.com, 7; Ljupco Smokovski/
Shutterstock.com, 9; Zack Frank/Shutterstock.com, 13;
mark reinstein/Shutterstock.com, 14–15;
Bumble Dee/Shutterstock.com, 17
Icons: © Aridha Prassetya/Dreamstime, 3, 5, 6, 13, 14,
17, 18, 22

ISBN HARDCOVER: 9781503827448
ISBN PAPERBACK: 9781622434459
LCCN: 2017961941

Printed in the United States of America
PA02379

About the Author

T.M. Merk is an elementary educator
with a master's degree in elementary
education from Lesley University in
Cambridge, Massachusetts. Drawing
on years of classroom experience, she
enjoys creating engaging educational
material that inspires students' passion
for learning. She lives in New Hampshire
with her husband and her dog, Finn.

Table of Contents

Touring with Toby

Toby's class went on a trip to Washington, D.C. They painted pictures of some of the **symbols** they saw.

Washington, D.C., is the capital of the United States of America. A capital usually has many monuments, museums, and memorials that teach about the country's history. In Washington, D.C., you can see America's founding documents, such as the Declaration of Independence and the U.S. Constitution, at the National Archives.

They stopped at a **memorial** to listen to a tour guide. Toby's friend started making funny faces. Toby laughed and made a silly face back.

Each country has its own flag. The flag is a symbol of the country. There are a few rules for respecting a flag. For example, you should always hold the flag up tall or fly it from a flagpole. In the United States, reciting the Pledge of Allegiance is a way to show respect for the flag and the country.

He forgot to listen to the tour guide.

Then he heard a voice. Leo the paintbrush was talking to him!

"Hey, Toby," Leo said. "The tour guide is teaching you about your country. Are you listening?"

"No, I guess not," Toby said.

"Then it's time to brush up on respect," Leo replied. "Learning about your country is important. There is a lot to learn about its symbols, leaders, and history. Try to focus on what the tour guide says. Knowing more about your country will help you learn to **respect** it."

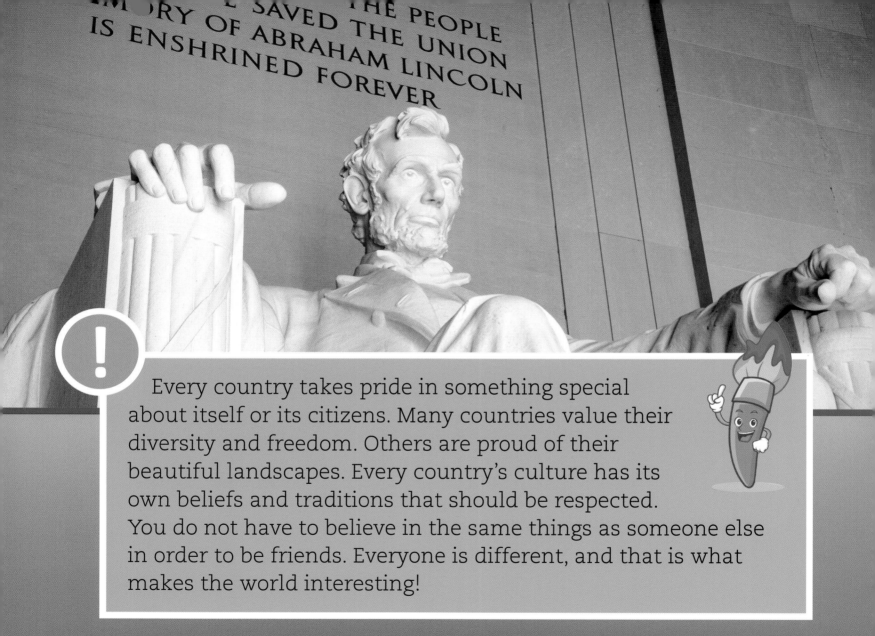

Every country takes pride in something special about itself or its citizens. Many countries value their diversity and freedom. Others are proud of their beautiful landscapes. Every country's culture has its own beliefs and traditions that should be respected. You do not have to believe in the same things as someone else in order to be friends. Everyone is different, and that is what makes the world interesting!

Many men and women serve in the military to protect a country and make sure that it can keep its freedoms. How can you honor them? In the United States, you can go to parades on Memorial Day and Veteran's Day. Those days are national holidays to respect and honor the men and women in the military.

"I'm sorry," Toby said. "What did I miss?"

"This is a memorial to honor the people who have served in the military," Leo said. "They protect our many **freedoms**. Memorials like this help us show respect for all the men and women who help our country."

"Wow," Toby said. He looked quietly at the memorial. "I think I will like learning about my country."

Leo smiled. "There are many ways to learn about it. You can even learn **patriotic** songs, like the national anthem!"

A national anthem is a country's official song. Most countries have an anthem. Some anthems are slow and serious, and others are fast and full of energy. An anthem is sung in its country's language. It is usually played on holidays, at ceremonies, and at the beginning of sporting events. If you know the words to an anthem, you can sing along. It is also respectful to quietly listen to a national anthem when it's played, even if it is the anthem of another country.

"The more I learn about my country, the more respect I have for it," Toby said. "I should go back to listening to the tour guide. Thanks!"

There are lots of things that you can do to be patriotic and show respect for your country. Everyone should do their part to be a good **citizen**. It is important to show that you care about your country's people, the land, and the rules of your government.

Respectful Talk

Do you need help talking in a respectful way about your country? Use these sentence starters to help!

- My country's history is important because ...

- People who serve in the military are heroes because ...

- I like my country because ...

- I should care about the land and the people of my country because ...

- I should learn about my country's symbols because ...

- I respect my country because ...

S.T.E.A.M. Activity

Build a Flagpole

Directions: Using only the materials provided, build a flagpole that stands up. You must attach the fabric to the pole to be the flag. The flagpole should stand up straight with the flag at the top.

Time Constraints: You may use a total of 25 minutes for your creation. You are allowed 10 minutes to plan and 15 minutes to build your flagpole. When you're done, make sure that it can stand up without being held.

Discussion: What did you do to make sure that the flagpole could stand up straight? Did your first plan work, or did you need to try again? What worked really well? What could you do better next time? When someone in your group was speaking, did you try to stay focused on him or her?

Suggested Materials:

- Small rectangle of fabric (to represent a flag)
- Tinfoil
- Popsicle sticks
- Toothpicks
- Tape
- Glue
- Safety scissors
- Markers/crayons

Glossary

citizen: (SIH-tuh-zin) A citizen is a person who lives in a country.

freedoms: (FREE-dumz) Freedoms are things that you are allowed to do.

memorial: (meh-MOR-ee-ul) A memorial is a structure created to honor someone or something.

patriotic: (pay-tree-AH-tik) When someone or something is patriotic, it shows love for its country.

respect: (rih-SPEKT) To respect is to show that you care about a person, place, thing, or idea.

symbols: (SIM-bulz) Symbols are pictures or objects that stand for something else.

To Learn More

Books

Loewen, Nancy. *We Live Here Too!: Kids Talk About Good Citizenship.* Minneapolis, MN: Picture Window Books, 2002.

Skeers, Linda. *The Impossible Patriotism Project.* New York, NY: Puffin Books, 2009.

Vigliano, Adrian. *Being a Good Citizen.* Chicago, IL: Heinemann Library, 2010.

Web Sites

Visit our Web site for links about respecting your country:
childsworld.com/links

Note to Parents, Teachers, and Librarians: We routinely verify our Web links to make sure they are safe and active sites. So encourage your readers to check them out!

Index